Garfield food for thought

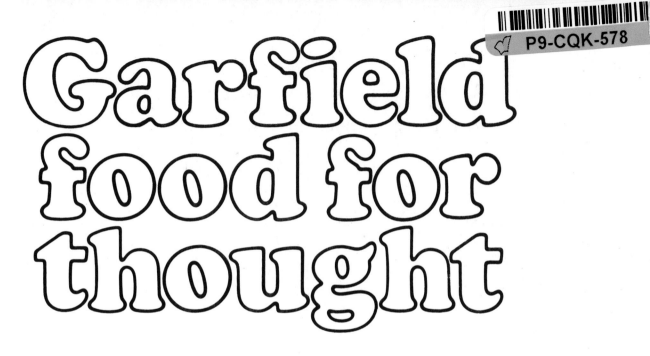

BY: JIM DAVIS

BALLANTINE BOOKS · NEW YORK

Library of Congress Catalog Card Number: 86-91556

ISBN: 0-345-34129-5

Manufactured in the United States of America

First Edition: March 1987

10 9 8 7 6 5 4 3 2 1

4

THESE NEW SODAS ARE GREAT

THEY'RE SUGAR-FREE AND CAFFEINE-FREE

AND FLAVOR-FREE

12

14

15

OKAY, SLURP, GO OUT AND FIND A COSTUME BEFITTING THE SIDEKICK OF THE CAPED AVENGER

8-30

RULE NUMBER ONE: NEVER DRESS BETTER THAN THE HERO

SLAP SLAP SLAP

JIM DAVIS

HERE COMES MY SIDEKICK, SLURP

ODIE

JIM DAVIS

CRASH!

HEY, SLURP, MAYBE YOU SHOULD CUT SOME EYEHOLES IN YOUR MASK

8-31

18

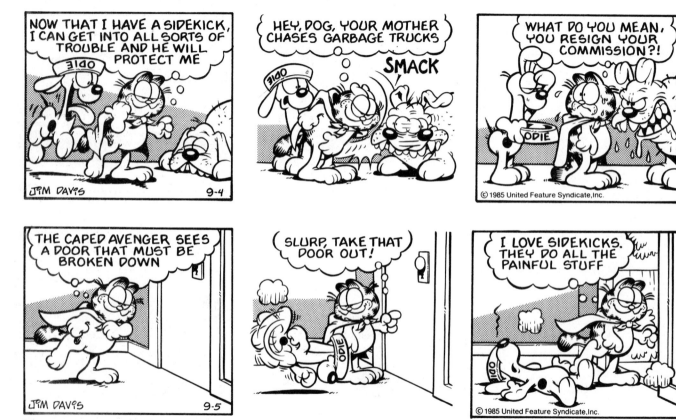

23

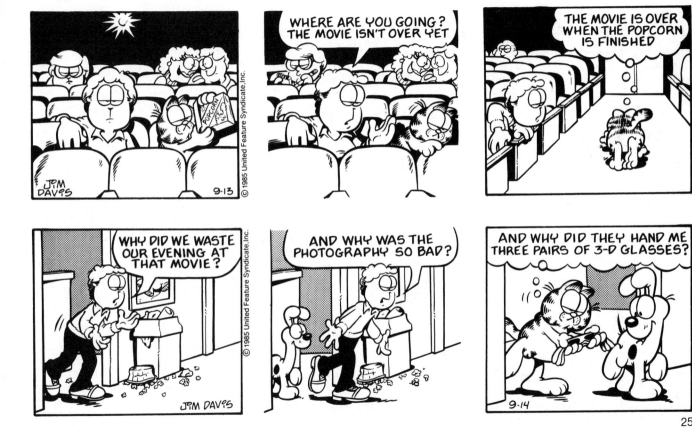

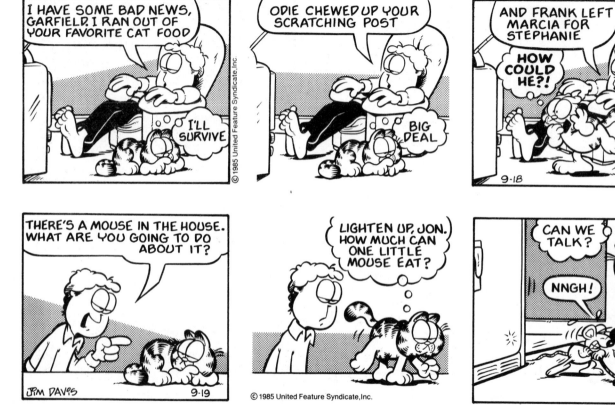

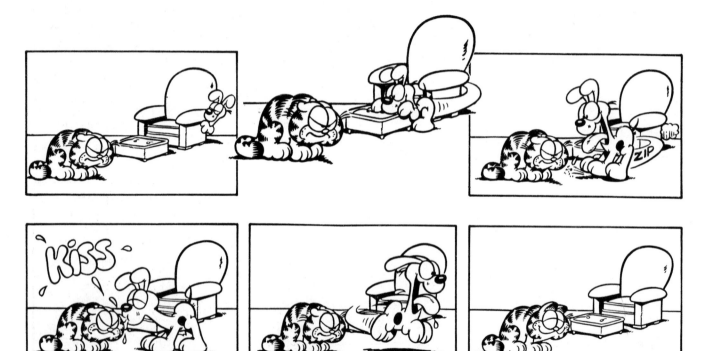

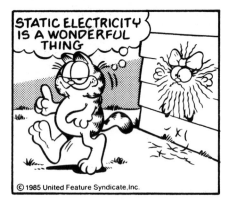

35

GARFIELD, YOU'RE SLEEPING YOUR LIFE AWAY

THERE'S A WHOLE WORLD OUT THERE FOR THE TAKING

GREAT. HAVE IT SENT TO MY BED

41

42

ARE YOU ASHAMED OF YOUR NEW BED, GARFIELD?

WHAT GIVES YOU THAT IDEA?

10-16

JON FINALLY GOT ME A BED WITH SOME CLASS

BUT IT'S JUST NOT ME. I HAVE MY PRIDE

AND PRIDE, OF COURSE, IS THE MIDDLE CLASS SUBSTITUTE FOR CLASS

10-17

45

46

KLANG!

© 1985 United Feature Syndicate, Inc.

OKAY! OKAY! YOU DIDN'T HAVE TO SHOUT

10-28

LET ME TELL YOU ABOUT MY MONDAY. MONDAY WAS GOING GREAT. I THOUGHT IT WAS GOING TO BE THE FIRST MONDAY OF MY LIFE THAT DIDN'T STINK

I GOT UP IN THE MIDDLE OF THE NIGHT AND ATE SOME JAWBREAKERS

© 1985 United Feature Syndicate, Inc.

THEN I WOKE UP THIS MORNING AND MY MARBLE COLLECTION WAS MISSING!

58

© 1985 United Feature Syndicate, Inc.

JPM DAVPS

11-10

65

66

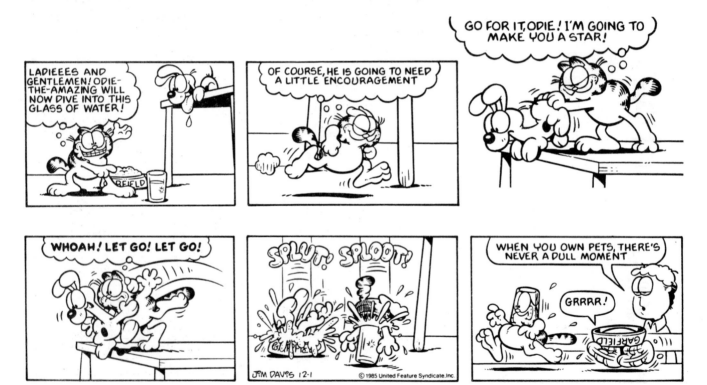

ODIE MUST BE GETTING SOMETHING OUT OF THIS WALL I'M NOT

© 1985 United Feature Syndicate, Inc. 12-6

I DON'T BELIEVE I FELL FOR THAT

© 1985 United Feature Syndicate, Inc. 12-7

84

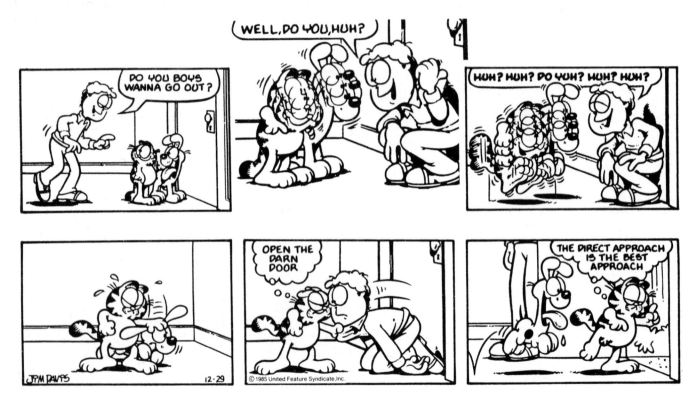

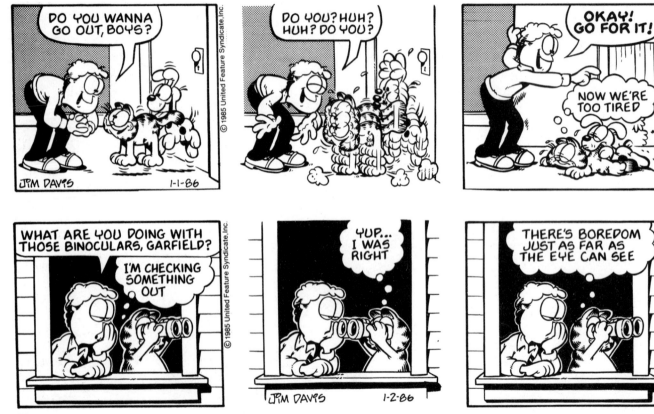

WE HAVE HERE THE LAST PIECE OF CAKE, GARFIELD

JIM DAVIS 1-17

I SUGGEST WE DRAW STRAWS TO SEE WHO GETS IT

I'M NOT A BETTING MAN

© 1986 United Feature Syndicate, Inc.

AND NOW THE WORLD-CLASS PANCAKE FLIPPER WILL DEMONSTRATE HIS SKILL

JIM DAVIS

© 1986 United Feature Syndicate, Inc.

PARDON MY IGNORANCE, MR. WORLD-CLASS PANCAKE FLIPPER, BUT SHOULDN'T THE STOVE BE TURNED ON FIRST?

1-18

98

99

GARFIELD'S Believe it, or DON'T!

IN 1957, A CAT IN OREGON SAVED A DROWNING CHILD

© 1986 United Feature Syndicate, Inc. 1-24

BUT, IT WAS UNDER THE LEGAL SIZE LIMIT, SO HE THREW THE KID BACK

Believe it, or DON'T!

JIM DAVIS

GARFIELD'S Believe it, or DON'T!

A CAT IN LUBBOCK, TEXAS GAVE BIRTH TO 57 KITTENS

© 1986 United Feature Syndicate, Inc.

WHEN ASKED HOW SHE FELT AFTER GIVING BIRTH TO QUINSEPTUPLETS, SHE SAID:

I'LL FEEL BETTER WHEN THEY START SLEEPING THROUGH THE NIGHT

JIM DAVIS 1-25

Believe it, or DON'T!

101

104

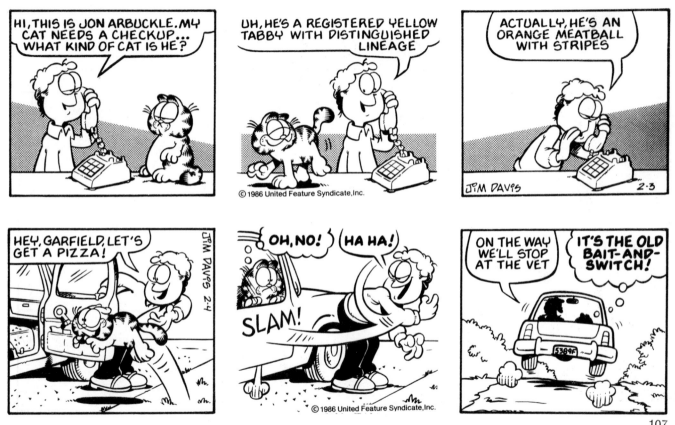

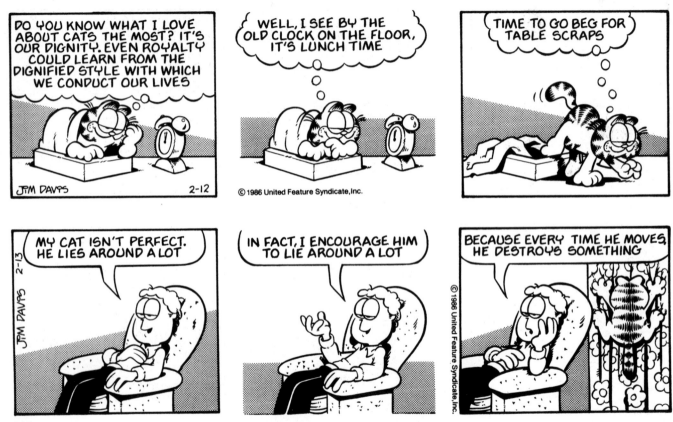

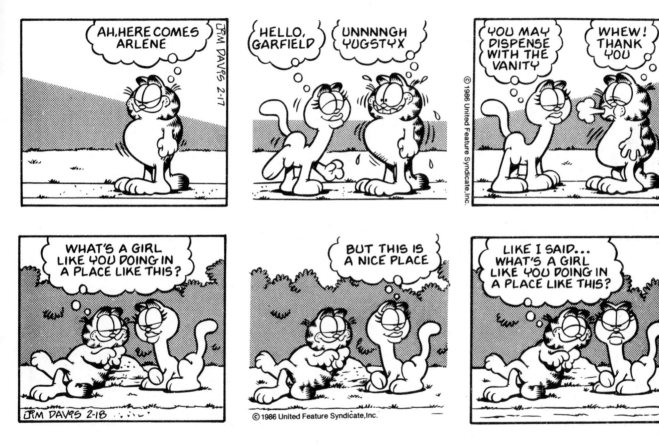

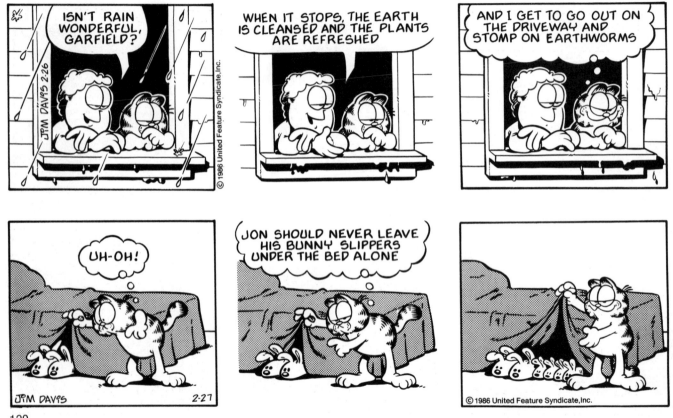

122